The Achievement Protocol

© 2018 Dennis Houchin

Reader Reviews

"This book is wonderful in helping me go in a new direction of being self-employed in the Information Technology (IT) world. The steps he has clearly laid out are extremely valuable in obtaining my short and my long term goals..."
- Beth, I.T. Consultant

"This is an awesome book. If you enjoy reading things like `The Four Agreements' and `Seven Habits' it's likely that you will find something of value in here. One highlight for me was the `Stanford Marshmallow Experiment', a study on delayed gratification..."
- Dana, Music Producer

"Thank you for this book! I have read many books and I am able to get little bits from each one to help me, but after reading "The Achievement Protocol" it is everything I have read plus more all in one place. I have gone from the mindset of "I will give it a try" to I will succeed."...
- Sabrina, Educator and Business Owner

"A positive, inspiring and practical way to understand the steps between understanding your purpose in life and actually accomplishing it."   - Josh Funk, Artist and Filmmaker

"I have been a fan of books like *Getting Things Done* (David Allen) for years, and I still learned something new from this book that will help me achieve my goals more effectively."
- Aaron Fisher, Magician & Creator

"Mr. Houchin brings a depth of understanding and creative enthusiasm for perfection in each area of his focus... This book is a quick read that should be revisited again and again as you build your future." - Marshall, Business Consultant

The Achievement Protocol

by which a person of any standing, wanting to accomplish great things, can achieve the greatest desires of their heart through its diligent application.

© 2018 Dennis Houchin

© 2018 Dennis Houchin

Ad Hoc Press

a division of
Ad Hoc Information Systems
P.O. Box 20
Gladeville, Tn. 37122

All rights reserved. No part of this publication may be reproduced, stored in a retrieval system, or transmitted in any form by any means electronic, mechanical, photocopying, recording or otherwise, without prior written permission of Ad Hoc Press. For permission to reproduce selected portions for any reason, please contact Ad Hoc Press at **inquiries@adhocpress.com**.

Publisher's Cataloging-in-Publication data
Houchin, Dennis, 1961-
   The Achievement Protocol / Dennis Houchin.
   p. cm.
   Includes bibliographical references and index.
   ISBN 978-0-9861205-0-3

1. Self actualization (Psychology). 2. Project management. I. Houchin, Dennis. 1961-. II. Title.
   158.1—dc23

MBTI® is a registered trademark of MBTI® Trust, Inc.
Post-It® is a registered trademark of 3M Corporation, Inc.
YouTube™ is a trademark of Google Inc. © 2012 Google Inc. All rights reserved.
   Rev. 1510.09

ABOUT THE AUTHOR

Dennis Houchin is a self-employed Information Technology consultant with over 35 years of experience in the Information Technology field. In 2011, he earned a Master of Science degree in Information Technology, specializing in Information Assurance and Security. He also has variety of technical and professional certifications. His specialties include Information System Design, Computer Network Design and Information System Security Design.

Dennis is also trained and certified in the non-technical discipline of administering and evaluating Myers-Briggs Type Indicator (MBTI®) personality assessments. He uses the MBTI® indicator with businesses to help individuals understand themselves better so that they can work more effectively together in teams.

Dennis speaks to national audiences of individuals and business owners and helps them recognize and remove the obstacles that stand in their path to a successful, fulfilling life.

DEDICATION

This book is dedicated to Terry, my wife of 39 years, and to my three children, each of them enabling me to live a life that has been filled with love and joy, although not devoid of the occasional pain and sorrow. They provide me with the inspiration and desire to become the best me that I can be.

CONTENTS

ABOUT THE AUTHOR V

DEDICATION VI

INTRODUCTION XI

PREFACE XIII

ACKNOWLEDGEMENTS XIX

WHAT YOU MUST KNOW BEFORE READING THIS BOOK! XXI

FOREWORD XXV

WHO WILL BENEFIT FROM THIS BOOK XXIX

TIPS FOR SUCCESS XXXI

UNDERSTANDING THE PATH AHEAD XXXIII

DEFINITIONS XXXVII

1 YOU CAN'T DO THAT! 1

2 CORE VALUES 5

3 VISIONS 11

    ACHIEVE SUCCESS BY LIVING A FULFILLING LIFE 15
    DISCOVERING YOUR PASSION 16
    DISCOVER HOW TO USE YOUR PASSION TO SERVE OTHERS 19
    MAKE IT EASY FOR SOMEONE TO PAY YOU FOR YOUR PASSION 22
    MANAGE EARNINGS WISELY AND REINVEST IN YOURSELF 23
    ENVELOPE SYSTEM 24
    SARAH 27
    WHAT IS YOUR VISION? 30

- Vision Summary 34

4 MISSIONS 37
- Mission Summary 42

5 PROJECTS AND SUBPROJECTS 43
- Defining Projects 45
- Project Summary 48

6 TASKS 49
- Examples of Tasks 52
- To Do Lists 54
- To-Do List Strategy 55
- Sarah's List 58
- Task Summary 64

7 MILESTONES 65
- Landmark Navigation 65
- Milestone Spacing 67
- Milestone Summary 68

8 REWARDS 69
- Delayed Gratification 71
- Reward Summary 73

9 REMINDERS 75
- Productivity Reminders 77
- Routine Reminders 78
- Tickler File 80
- Reminder Summary 81

10 ROADBLOCKS 83

Choosing the Wrong Vision		84
Life is Organic		85
Stress		88
Fear of Failure		94
Fear of Success		95
Fear of Criticism		97
Time Flies		99
Roadblock Summary		101
11	**DESPERATION & INSPIRATION**	**103**
Desperation		103
Inspiration		107
Desperation and Inspiration Summary		108

CONCLUSION 109

AFTERWORD 113

INDEX 117

APPENDIX 120

- Vision Worksheet 121
- Mission Worksheet 122
- Project Task List 123
- Evening Review 124
- Daily To-Do List 125
- Daily To-Do List 126
- Progress Tracking 127

REFERENCES 128

The Achievement Protocol

INTRODUCTION

Traveling
'The Road Less Traveled'

*No amount of travel on the wrong road,
will bring you to the right destination.*

Ben Gaye, III

Sometimes the *Road Less Traveled* is less traveled because it leads nowhere. But more often, the "Road Less Traveled" is less traveled because it requires more effort than most people are willing to expend. It's less traveled because it requires more courage than most people can muster. It's less traveled because it involves more risk than most people think they can tolerate.

Yet the *Road Less Traveled* is the very road upon which all leaders, be they persons or organizations, eventually travel. The questions that these leaders must answer before embarking upon their journey, and at various times along their journey, is this: How do we ensure that the road before us is not the wrong road? How can we be sure that this road will lead us to our destination?

The following pages will help answer that question. The system presented in this book is a practical guide with easy to follow steps that anyone can use to remove some of the confusion that often confronts us as we strive for a life that has meaning.

> *Two roads diverged in a wood, and I -*
> *I took the one less traveled by,*
> *And that has made all the difference.*
>
> *Robert Frost*

PREFACE

I was standing in the kitchen one day talking with my daughter, Kristina. She was a senior in college at the time and active in the National Model United Nations program. We were discussing her organizational skills.

She is extremely busy, and extremely productive, and extremely organized, but even she was feeling frustrated about staying on top of all of the classes, working groups, meetings, and deadlines that were in front of her. She commented that many of her peers had similar problems.

Kristina and her friends all used a variety of tools to track tasks and deadlines, but they were not always effective. Of course, many of her friends also spent a lot of time in pursuits that were not necessarily germane to their futures or their course of study. They found creative ways to squander their time, which naturally increased the level of stress they were under.

Coincidentally, I had just completed a long-term consulting assignment as Chief Information Officer for a technologically diverse private company and was brainstorming ideas for a new development project.

Some of the skills that I had developed over the years were *strategic management*, *project management* and *time management*. Strategic management is used to define the long-range vision for a business, and to create appropriate plans for achieving the vision. Project management is being able to break complex projects down into their component tasks, identify the necessary resources and responsibilities and set and meet deadlines. Time management is about setting priorities and maximizing the use of the time that is available to you.

Using sound *strategic management*, *project management* and *time management techniques* aided me not only in my career and in building an independent information technology consulting company, but it also enabled to me to complete two college degrees in addition to studying for and earning numerous industry and vendor certifications.

I had been thinking about creating an app that would be useful and helpful to a broad spectrum of people, so while we were having that conversation in the kitchen, is was natural for Kristina to suggest that I write an app to solve the organizational and prioritization problems that she and her friends all seemed to be having.

After doing some research and initiating the process of designing the app, it soon became apparent that effective usage of the app was going to require a working understanding of time management, project management, and strategic management principles. This book will lay out those principles.

As I began to reflect on how my knowledge in these areas had developed over the course of my life, I realized that these disciplines were really the means to an end. An end that I had conceived of many years ago.

I first began thinking about success and achievement in the late 1970's. I was a high school drop-out and had already spent a number of years abusing my brain with intoxicants. I had no discernible talents or prospects for the future, beyond menial labor.

As I began to study success and achievement and started to achieve success in my own life, I committed myself to helping others find their path to success, whenever possible.

I have counselled, encouraged, and supported various individuals that I have encountered over the past three decades, including my own children. I have encouraged them to find their own path, and pursue what they truly love.

So standing in the kitchen that day, it became clear that I was in the right place at the right time to help others find not only the answers to their daily organizational struggles, but ultimately their path to fulfillment. At the same time I was fulfilling one of my own visions that I had formed almost four decades ago.

May the ideas in this book serve you as well as they have served me.

Dennis Houchin, December 2014

The Achievement Protocol

ACKNOWLEDGEMENTS

A book of this nature is not written in isolation. Many people, far too numerous to mention, have contributed to the experiences from which this book is drawn. This work is my interpretation of what I have learned from my various influences.

I would first like to acknowledge, Hugh Van Cleve, sadly no longer with us, for the inspiration, instruction, opportunity, and encouragement that he provided to me in my early career.

Many friends, who are also successful entertainers, artists, instructors and entrepreneurs, have contributed quality thoughts and suggestions that have helped me shape this book into a form that I feel will be most helpful to you.

I would like to specifically acknowledge the kindness and generosity of Dr. Edwin A. Locke, the co-founder of goal-setting theory, who provided personal comments, insight, and reference material to me as I brought this book into its final form. It is a considerably better book as a result of our discussions.

The collaborative work of Edwin Locke and Gary Latham in the late 1960's regarding goal setting and task motivation, followed by more than four decades of research and dedication to the subject, laid the foundation for what would become a significant factor in improving global organizational productivity.

But most of all, I want to acknowledge my family, who has put up with all the various inconveniences that accompany my fits of creative endeavor.

Finally, I would like to thank my oldest son, Wayne Houchin for writing the Afterword for this edition. Wayne used the ideas presented in this book to create the life of his dreams and with now more than 20 years of experience as a professional magician, inventor and entrepreneur, has proven the power of living a life of passion. Visit http://bonus.adhocpress.com for additional information and free resources to supplement the materials in this book.

WHAT YOU MUST KNOW BEFORE READING THIS BOOK!

There will be parts of this book that you absolutely love! You will want to sit down and write the author and thank him for the great insight! And then there will be sections that you really, really don't love. At all. You will wonder if it was even worth the time to spend reading the book and you will be tempted to skip over these parts. There is a very good reason for this. This book has been intentionally constructed to present two equally important points of view for you to consider as you work through this system.

The Achievement Protocol

This system will take you through exercises and introduce you to processes that involve broad, sweeping, conceptual ideas. Less than half the world really loves looking at the 'big picture' in non-specific terms and dealing with life at a high level. It will also take you through very detailed, highly structured exercises - which are preferred by just over half of the world.

The power of this system lies in using both approaches, both modes of thought, to guide you along a path of fulfillment and self-actualization, to help you become all that you are meant to be.

As you encounter sections of this book that you find uncomfortable, celebrate! Because you have just found an area in which you are about to grow. I encourage you to pay particular attention to those areas that may not represent your preferred mode of thought. When you develop some skill in the areas that you find most challenging, you will find that your efforts will be rewarded beyond measure. You will find that you are able to achieve things that you never thought possible.

Some of you may already have learned to integrate these different modes of thought and you will likely find it easier to see the value of this system and to start putting it into practical use.

While the ideas presented in this book are simple and easy to understand, they may prove to be more difficult to implement for some. For those of you that are new on this path of seeking to live a fulfilled life, set your vision then let that be your guiding light.

When your vision is clear, when you know where you target is and you know that it is worthwhile and consistent with your core values, the difficulties you encounter along the way will seem trivial when compared with the ultimate value of the results to be achieved.

The Achievement Protocol

FOREWORD

The Achievement Protocol is a priceless gift. A Treasure of Truth that shows you, step-by-step, that you can pursue your passion and make it an integral part of your life. It is a clearly detailed map that teaches you that living out the life you love most is well within your capability to achieve.

It's been said that the two most important days of your life are the day you were born, and the day you finally know WHY.

As a human, you were born to grow, to become who you are meant to be. For that to happen, a seed is growing in your being that makes you feel you are constantly restless. You feel uneasy, uncomfortable or even unaware, of a situation or dilemma that causes a previously unknown hunger within you to grow daily.

This is no ordinary hunger, it's the hunger of knowing that you were born to Be So Much More.

We are often held back because we see our lives against the background of our environment, heredity, and personal history. Thankfully as time passes, your personal hunger for Meaning & Purpose far outweighs all the excuses you can ever come up with that prevent you from growing up to become the Greatest Person you were born to be.

The discomfort you feel is a gift. There is some kind of beautiful polarity in your life that is pulling in different directions and causing stress.

It's a deep longing, a yearning yet undefined that draws you to go on a life-changing adventure. As blessings tend to do, the hunger refuses to go away.

By reading, and actively doing the exercises found herein, you will find you have been gifted with a clearly written, well-traveled, heavily & wisely annotated, map whose purpose is to help you bridge the gap between where you are today and where your life shall be when everything you do comes from loving and appreciating the unique miracle that you are.

By choosing to bring to life what you love, you get to partake fully of all the blessings you were born to receive.

The information found in The Achievement Protocol will help you clearly identify what it is that you are passionate about achieving. Under its guidance, you will discover how to satisfy your hunger. How to live your Purpose.

Ozzie Coto, January 2015

The Achievement Protocol

WHO WILL BENEFIT FROM THIS BOOK

This book is not for everyone. People who are already living happy, successful lives and describe themselves as fulfilled or self-actualized; who are already on track to achieve the results of a life lived with intention, may find this book of interest, but will probably not benefit very much.

This book is not for those who are content with their current life and do not wish to change or discover whether they have a greater purpose to fulfill.

However, for those who struggle with accomplishing daily tasks or feel like they are wasting their time; who have not yet discovered their life purpose, or who have struggled in frustration while trying to achieve their life purpose will find this book to be a great help. This book will map out a step by step process that will assure that you not only do things right, but that you also do the right things to shape and mold your life in a way that will ultimately bring success and fulfillment to your life.

This book will be as helpful to serious minded high school students that are trying to find their direction, as it is to college students trying to excel and maintain their sanity, as it is to adults that may find that they are not satisfied with their current direction, or even to citizens of advanced age and experience that find themselves beginning a new phase of life.

Regardless of where you are in life, or what your past has been, if you are longing for a more fulfilling future, this book can help you forge the path that is right for you.

TIPS FOR SUCCESS

To get the most value out of this book, I suggest you read all the way through once, armed with the following materials: Pencil, Highlighter, Post-it® Notes. Make notes in the book as you read through it. Whenever you see the symbol at the right, write the answer to the question on a separate Post-It note. Keep the note on the same page, or transfer it to another folder or the back of the book.

Then after reading the last page, and after you've seen the entire process, go through the book again and use the tools found in the appendix to begin the transformative process that will bring you happiness and success.

The Achievement Protocol

UNDERSTANDING THE PATH AHEAD

I n the following pages we are going to explore a comprehensive multi-layered system that has been developed by the author. Many of the components of this system have existed for thousands of years and have been written about by many other authors. The ideas are culled from proven techniques in the fields of strategic planning, goal setting, project management, and personal performance optimization. This system is unique because it brings together the most essential elements required for the process of achieving fulfillment in a comprehensive manner that to date has not been so thoroughly explained in such a complete system.

This book will show you specific steps that you can use to attain a happy and fulfilled life. This book will show you how to overcome any obstacle in pursuit of that fulfillment. As you do those things that are necessary to achieve fulfillment, you may earn more riches than you can imagine, if that is part of what you are seeking. However this book will not show you how to visualize a million dollars into existence. It will not show you how to double your money in seven days. There are other books that will make those claims. What you *will* get in this book is a methodology that will help you develop a solid plan that will lead you on the most direct path possible to achieving your dreams, achieving the visions that represent your unique purpose in this life.

Before we begin discussing those dreams and the visions that you will strive for, we will first explore your core values, which are central to determining whether achieving your vision will actually be fulfilling. Then, visualizing the system as a pyramid, we will start at the very top. At the apex of the pyramid we discuss your ultimate vision, then step by step we will work down the pyramid until we reach the foundation which consists of the actions you take on a daily or even hourly basis.

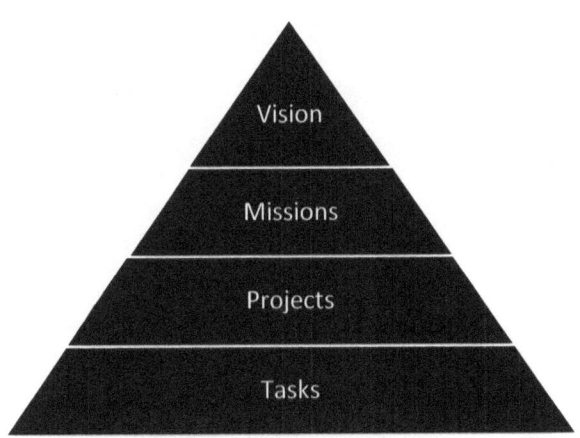

The Achievement Protocol

DEFINITIONS

In goal setting and achievement literature there is often confusion around the way that some of the words are used. For clarity in this system, these are the definitions used throughout this book:

Core Values	*A core value is a deeply held value or belief that is inherent in a vision. It is a guiding principle that is held in the deepest part of your being.* In the case of NASA it might be "Man is capable of going to the moon". The core value tends to be passive, while the vison is active.	Criminal Defense is an integral part of Justice System and must be vigorously protected.
Vision	*An idealized final state, typically sweeping in scope and fairly imprecise. It represents the pinnacle of all of your efforts.* For example: The vision of NASA in 1961 was to land a man on the moon and return him safely to earth.	Become a successful Criminal Defense Attorney.
Mission or Goal	*For any Vision or Core Value, you will have one or more Missions that bring that Vision into reality or demonstrate the truth of the Core Value.* For example, NASA had many missions: Develop engineers and pilots; develop aircraft to test theories, develop training equipment and procedures; Develop control	Obtain Law Degree from Columbia University. Develop relationships with High Profile Defense Attorneys Obtain Undergraduate Degree from Mam's Alma Mater.

The Achievement Protocol

	technology, Develop detailed execution plans, etc.	
Project	*Each Mission will consist of one or more projects. A project has a defined end result, specific time frame, and list of discrete tasks.* Examples of NASA might be: Create manufacturing plan for Solid Fuel rocket engine, Create Test Procedure for Solid Fuel rocket engine	Complete this semesters classes with 4.0 GP Actively participate in Debate Club Challenge Professors with thoughtful and valuable questions
Tasks	*Each Project has multiple tasks associated with it. Each task is a discrete action to be taken which leads to the completion of a project.* For one of NASA's projects we might see: Create Chemical Formula for Solid Fuel rocket engine, Test formula in various conditions and record results; Create Draft Manufacturing Plan for Review, Edit Draft Manufacturing Plan, Submit Draft for Final Review, Create Final Edition of Approved Manufacturing Plan	Devote 9 hours of study outside of class each day Get at least 5 hours of sleep Spend no more than 2.5 hours daily in meal time Socialize no more than 90 minutes a day (outside of mealtime) Attempt to exceed requirements for each assignment
Milestones	Milestones are specific conditions in the project and dates at which you expect to see those conditions. They can be attached to Missions, Goals, Projects or Tasks	Ace 4 straight weeks of quizzes in every class. Earn better than 90% on mid-terms
Reminders	Reminders are set to occur at various intervals and can be attached to Missions, Goals, Projects, Tasks or Milestones,	Daily – reminders about specific assignments, study time Weekly – reminder to review previous week's work and preview next week's work
Rewards	These are rewards that you attach to Milestones that will be granted if the milestone is reached by the specified date.	Have night out with friends at 4 week milestone (3 drink maximum) Take trip on weekend and forget about school until Sunday night at mid-term milestone

1 YOU CAN'T DO THAT!

"You definitely have a knack for this and your class performance is great, but you should reconsider your decision to pursue this professionally. It's a very competitive field and you probably will not fare very well."

Have you ever been told that you can't do something that you love to do? Have you been told that you'll never be successful if you pursue your passion?

The words quoted in the first paragraph were spoken to me by a college professor. He was talking about the Information Technology field, and specifically, computer programming. These words, from a professor and advisor that I respected, were jarring to me. He was telling me that the one career that I was passionate about was not appropriate for me. Now, 36 years after that advice, I don't remember the names of my other professors at Northern Arizona University in Flagstaff, Arizona, but I will always remember his name.

Within 6 months of hearing that advice from the computer programming professor who was also assigned to me as my academic counselor, I was working professionally as a database programmer for a local office products retailer. In less than a year, I was working as the junior programmer for a computer company, and within 8 months I was transferred to Tucson to open a new branch office as the senior programmer and manager of the software department. We developed, installed, and supported custom applications for businesses. I continued to grow and develop in my profession.

In 1988 I relocated to Northern California, working with a team to develop custom business applications, and in 1994 I opened the doors to my own Information Technology consulting business in Chico, California. In 2014 I celebrated the 20th year of operating that business.

In the 35 years that I've spent in this "very competitive field" that an expert told me to abandon, my wife and I have raised 3 children to be independent, successful, and fulfilled as they pursue their own dreams.

Living an exciting, fulfilling life is something that any of us can do, but it is something that many of us, myself included, have struggled with.

In the following pages I will share with you the techniques that I have learned that have enabled me, and will enable you, to discover and pursue your passion in a way that not only leads to a fulfilling achievement, but also provides a fulfilling experience along the way.

Beginning with understanding Core Values you will learn the concrete tools that are essential to a fulfilled life

2 CORE VALUES

Your beliefs become your thoughts. Your thoughts become your words. Your words become your actions. Your actions become your habits. Your habits become your values. Your values become your destiny.
Mahatma Gandhi

Core values are those deeply held conscious or subconscious beliefs that form the essence of our character. Core values may be partially innate and partially learned. They are typically formed very early in life. It is possible to change core values, but change typically comes very slowly and the changes tend to be lasting.

We can learn Core Values, which form our individual morality, from religious upbringing, family or social traditions, or from ethical systems such as that afforded by the Objectivism of Ayn Rand. Core values can be open, aspirational, expansive and positive:

- The Universe is fundamentally good
- Strangers are just friends you've never met
- It is wrong to lie
- It is wrong to kill other people
- Be a thoughtful steward of your resources

Core values can also be closed, restricted and negative. Some examples include:

- I am not likable
- Only people from my [family, group, tribe, organization, club, gang] are worthy of my kindness
- It doesn't matter if others get hurt, as long as I get what I want
- Only naïve fools always tell the truth, you have to lie to get ahead
- I'm more important than anyone else

Core values, whether positive or negative often exist as unquestioned assumptions and affect many aspects of our lives. We sometimes hold them without recognizing them or recognizing how they color our experience of the world.

Core values are integral to creating an attainable vision, even though they are often assumed and not stated explicitly. For example, if your vision is "Discover a cure for cancer", you may have one or more of the following core values:

- Pain and disease (including Cancer) can and should be eliminated from the world
- It is possible for a cure to be discovered by a person
- You have the potential to be the person that discovers the cure
- Finding a cure is a noble use of one's life

Take special note of third core value in this list, "You have the potential to be the person that discovers the cure". If a person does not have such a core value, or if she has the opposite as a core value, then their actions will eventually reflect that value and they will eventually end their search for a cure in frustration, because they are convinced they will not be able to be successful.

It is not uncommon for us to hold core values such as this one that limit us in some way. When we have a deeply held belief that we are incapable of passing beyond some perceived limitation, then we will not be able to pass beyond that limitation. I recall a story often told by the great Zig Ziglar (1974) regarding the training of fleas.

The essence of the story was this: if you take some fleas and put them in a jar then put the lid on the jar, you can watch the fleas jumping in an attempt to get out. As they jump they will bump the lid and fall back down. They will do this repeatedly. After a while you'll begin to notice that the fleas are still jumping but they are not quite reaching the lid. They've found their comfort zone! The area that they can move in without banging their head. If you then take the lid off of the jar, the fleas will not jump out. So ingrained is the belief that they cannot go further, that they will not be able to jump high enough to clear the edge of the jar.

People behave similarly – allowing our core beliefs to artificially determine our limitations, not realizing that by simply changing the core belief we remove the artificial limitation.

Dr. Albert Bandura (2013), in *New Developments in Goal Setting and Task Performance,* describes three specific areas in which our core beliefs about our ability, or our *self-efficacy*, can limit or regulate our performance; How well we think we can overcome obstacles, how well we think we can resist external pressure or temptation, and how well we think we can do the job required.

We tend to live up to, or down to, our own expectations about our ability. Henry Ford is credited with saying "Whether you think you can, or think you can't – you're right!"

It is important to have alignment between your vision and your core values. Otherwise we may end up subconsciously creating conditions that make it more difficult to achieve our vision.

Let's assume, for example, that based on input from teachers, your parents, society or some other influence, you have consciously determined that the best thing you could do with your life is cure cancer, so you select that as your vision. Now let's also assume that you were convinced at a very young age that if a person has cancer, it is because they ate red meat. This belief would certainly affect your approach to curing cancer and may cause you to disregard some new potentially helpful information that did not fit with your existing belief.

This phenomenon, zeroing in on information that supports our existing belief and dismissing information that challenges our existing belief is known as confirmation-bias and can play a significant role in how we view and interact in our world.

In the next section we will begin to discuss your vision. As you create each vision think honestly about the core values that you currently have that might influence your ability to achieve the vision. If you find core values that you need to change, or ones that you don't have, but should, write them down on the back of the post-note.

Take your time with this exercise. The more candid thought you give to this part of the process, the better the selected vision will fit your life.

3 VISIONS

Someone's sitting in the shade today because someone planted a tree a long time ago.

Warren Buffet

Vision is essential to living a fulfilled life. Or more accurately, having a vision is essential to living a fulfilled life, because the sense of fulfillment comes not only when the vision is attained, but also as we see ourselves making progress toward the vision.

The word vision, as it used in this system, is what you ultimately want to achieve in life. An important distinction here is that it reflects what you want *to achieve*, not necessarily what you want *to have*. I make that distinction because we are often told to start our long range thinking, by looking at what we want to have or what we want to get. By thinking instead about what we want to achieve, we will find that what we end up having will be in line with what we achieve.

Although financial goals can and should be a part of what you seek, in order to have a fulfilling life, you need a Vision that is more reflective of how you want to spend your time. It is possible for an artist, an auto-mechanic, a doctor, a magician, or a union laborer to have a successful, fulfilling life regardless of how high or how low their net worth, provided they are spending their time pursuing a vision that is consistent with their core values and they are managing whatever income they earn responsibly.

It's often helpful to think of it in terms of what you would like to be remembered for when you leave this earth. Imagine what you would want to be said about you in your obituary or on your headstone. It does not have to be terribly specific, and in fact, may change and develop as you change and develop.

- "John was a faithful husband and good father."
- "Susan broke down societal barriers and pioneered a solution to world hunger."
- "Jason developed the first practical and affordable cure for cancer."
- "Sarah was a brilliant painter, sculptor, mathematician and choreographer."

These statements all contain reasonable Visions that can be worked toward over the course of your lifetime.

But our lives are multifaceted. An individual may have a separate vision for each area of their life. For example, they may have a vision for family, a vision for career, a vision for education, and a vision for their spiritual life. In any particular area they would have only one over-arching vision. If it seems like you have multiple visions in one area, then you should consider a vision that is large enough to contain both.

In other words, if you have the vision of obtaining a Master's degree in Chemistry and another vision of obtaining a PHD in biology, you could combine those into one like this, "Obtain multiple advanced degrees in multiple sciences."

The vision should reflect not only what you are able to accomplish now, but what you would like to be able to accomplish someday. The visions should represent those things that *you* love, not what someone else thinks you 'ought to' love.

Achieve Success by Living a Fulfilling Life

I have often said that there are really only four essential requirements for anyone to achieve great success:

- Discover your passion, what you love to do
- Discover how you can use your passion to serve other people
- Make it simple for people to pay you to do what you love to do
- Manage whatever you earn wisely and reinvest in yourself

These four elements are simple, though not necessarily easy. However, while there may be some difficulty along the way, if you get the first requirement right, you will not regret the effort it takes to accomplish the other three.

If your vision consists of something that you love, you will find joy and happiness in every sore muscle, every drop of sweat, and every scar that brings its realization closer to you.

Discovering Your Passion

For many of us, this is the most difficult of these simple requirements. Discovering what you love, what you are most passionate about, often requires honest self-reflection and self-awareness. It also requires some life experiences.

Sometimes the thing that you love; the idea, principle, or action that you are most passionate about, shows up unexpectedly in your life. You may be inspired by a particular speaker or life event, co-worker, boss, or fellow student. The good news is that when you encounter it, you will probably recognize it. You will feel a genuine enthusiasm at the prospect of achieving it, even when you reflect that the road may not always be smooth and straight. The word 'enthusiasm' comes from Greek roots and means literally to be possessed by God. When we are enthusiastic about something, we are driven by an energy and a power that we do not seem to have in other times. It is this energy that propels us to carry on though obstacles and tough times.

Many people have difficulty believing they can pursue their passion and make it an integral part of their life. It is not uncommon for someone to think that they aren't good enough or deserving enough or capable enough to pursue their passion. Our society tends to find it easier to deal with people that fit nicely into neat little boxes. It takes some effort to break out of that thinking and to commit to pursuing *the road less traveled*.

Not all visions are related to career. You can have visions for a variety of areas in your life, which we will discuss more fully in a few pages.

When you think about your vision regarding your career, it's important to remember that in almost any passion you might want to pursue, there are probably already examples of people who have been successful doing it, and even if something has never been done before does not mean it can never be done. For everything that has been done, there was someone that was the first to do it. Maybe you were meant to be the first person to succeed at your particular passion.

The techniques and processes you will find in this book are intended to help you pursue your passion whatever you determine it to be.

If you already have that passion and would like guidance on effectively and efficiently pursuing that passion, then the rest of this book will help provide you with the tools you need.

If you are at the very beginning of this exciting journey, then you will need to take some time and try to identify just what it is that you are passionate about achieving. What are those ideas that fill you with enthusiasm? I'm reminded of these words:

> *Enthusiasm is one of the most powerful engines of success. When you do a thing, do it with all your might. Put your whole soul into it. Stamp it with your own personality. Be active, be energetic, be enthusiastic and faithful, and you will accomplish your object. Nothing great was ever achieved without enthusiasm*
>
> *Ralph Waldo Emerson.*

Discover How to Use your Passion to Serve Others

It is a universal law, that you will be rewarded for the value that you are able to give to others. If you want to earn money with your passion, you need to figure out how to use that passion to serve others. The most important thing I want you to take away from this section is this: Nearly ANYTHING that you can be passionate about can be used to serve others. Let's look at some examples.

Let's say you're passionate about something like… chocolate! You might at first think "I can't serve anyone by eating chocolate". But don't chocolate manufacturers have tasters that they hire? What would stop you from working for a chocolate company? But you may be *really* passionate about chocolate. Not just eating it, but smelling it, knowing it's origin and history, it's manufacturing process, the parts of the world that make different types of chocolate. Why not study it in depth and become a chocolate expert, speaking at conventions, writing books, and magazine or journal articles. Or work for a chocolate company in their research and development division. Or apply for grants from private companies, organizations, medical institutions, academic institutions, etc., so you can do in depth studies on chocolate. As long as there are people that like to eat chocolate, you can bet that someone that is passionate about chocolate will be able to find a way to use that passion to serve someone else, and in so doing earn a respectable living that is fulfilling beyond measure.

Maybe chocolate isn't your thing. Maybe it's beer instead. Read the above paragraph substituting the word 'chocolate' with 'beer'.

Even if your passion is sitting still and doing absolutely nothing! You can probably find someone that is researching slothfulness, or a furniture manufacturer that needs a way to measure how comfortable the various models of chairs are and how long a person can sit before it becomes too uncomfortable, or an art school that needs live models.

I am personally aware of at least three individuals that turned their passion for playing video games into lucrative careers in the gaming industry.

So if you have thought no one would be interested in what you have to offer, I would encourage you to think again. You may have to move, or change some habits, but somewhere out there you will be able to find people that wish they had exactly what you have to passionately offer to them. Find those people.

MAKE IT EASY FOR SOMEONE TO PAY YOU FOR YOUR PASSION

Unless there is already an established job market for people that are doing whatever you are passionate about, you will need to make it easy for those you serve to pay you or hire you. Be clear about what you have to offer. Create an elevator pitch – a brief description of what you do that is concise and clear enough that you can communicate it to someone else in the space of an elevator ride – 30 seconds or so. Know what your service is worth. This may be hard in the beginning if you're starting off in a new field, but keep adjusting your prices until you have a good idea about what people will pay for your service. If what you're doing isn't very unique, then do some research to find out what others get paid.

Be prepared to answer two questions that you will be asked: What can you do for me; and how much will it cost?

MANAGE EARNINGS WISELY AND REINVEST IN YOURSELF

Second to figuring out what your passion is, this the most difficult for a lot of people. There an old bit of practical wisdom that says that everybody is controlled. You either choose to control yourself, or someone else will control you. This is particularly apt here when it comes to managing what you earn. If you are prudent, live within your means, and reinvest in yourself to make yourself the best at delivering your passion, you will be successful.

On the other hand, if you choose not to use self-control, then you will be setting the stage to be governed by debt and by poor decision making. There are many resources available that will help you manage your earnings. Take advantage of these so that you will be able to devote your time to pursuing your passion, which is what you really want to do.

One of these resources is a budgeting tool known as the Envelope System, the subject of our next section.

Envelope System

When my wife and I were married in 1979, my grandfather gave me a manuscript, written by a friend of his, for a book that described a system of managing personal finances called The Envelope System. It is now a very popular system that you can easily find on the internet. There are many financial gurus and advisors that recommend the system, including Dave Ramsey. I believe there's even an app for that now.

The system has been extremely effective for my family and for everyone that I know that has put it into practice.

The essence of the system is that when you get paid, or receive some sort of income, rather than let it sit in your checking account, you divide the money up and put the cash into a series of envelopes. Each envelope contains all the money that you can spend on that item. For example, let's say that you normally spend $350 per month on groceries and you get paid twice a month. When you deposit your paycheck you keep $175 dollars out in cash, and put that into your envelope. Then when you buy groceries, you can only use the money that is in the groceries envelope.

For expenses that don't happen every month, like insurance or car repair or clothing, you calculate or estimate what the expense for the year will be, then divide it by twelve to come up with your monthly amount, then make sure that each month you are putting that amount into the envelope. When your insurance comes due, or when you need to update your winter wardrobe, you can use the money from the appropriate envelopes. These types of 'hidden' expenses were particularly difficult for my wife and me early on. We would go along thinking that we were doing ok, then suddenly an insurance bill that is paid every six months would come due, or we'd have to buy new tires for the car and it would put a major stress on our family. When we started using the envelope system and accounting for these other expenses that don't occur every month, it was much easier for us to get on top of our finances.

Here's how to get started.

Make a list of each item that you spend money on – rent, food, clothes, fuel, utilities, books, phone, insurance, savings etc. Don't forget the other expenses that may not occur every single month.

For each item on your list, write the name down on an envelope. Then each time you get a paycheck or receive income, take the money and distribute it among the envelopes, according to your budget.

If you are self-employed, be sure to have an envelope for taxes that you will need to pay. Taxes are an expense that you can predict, but cannot control and neglecting them can come at a high cost.

In the next section, I'm going to tell you the story of Sarah, a fictitious character, and illustrate what these principles look like when you see them in action. We will learn more about Sarah as we proceed through this book.

Sarah

Let me introduce you to Sarah. Sarah was a freshman college student. She was attending a State University, but was not sure what she wanted to study. Her parents thought she should go into Social Psychology, but Sarah wasn't convinced that she wanted to do that.

Sara grew up in a large family with 3 younger brothers and a younger sister. Her mother and father worked long hours, so as she got older, she took on more responsibility for planning and cooking family meals. She loved to cook and became quite creative at preparing excellent meals for a large group of people using vegetables from her garden and making economical purchases at the Farmer's Market and the local grocery store.

Sarah was very organized and took meticulous notes regarding her meals. She loved to scan the internet for new recipes and new ideas. She often fantasized about having a restaurant and a YouTube™ channel where she could teach cooking.

Sarah came across a copy of The Achievement Protocol. She was intrigued by the title so she looked at the back cover and realized that maybe she didn't have to settle for a degree in Social Psychology. Maybe there was something better waiting for her.

Sarah began applying The Achievement Protocol. She decided her vision was to be a world famous chef, travelling the world and teaching internationally. She concluded that in doing this, she would be able to help individuals learn how to cook really great, healthy meals, and she would also be helping restaurants learn the techniques that would let them better serve their customers and thereby increase their revenue. After several days of thinking about what would be required, she decided that she would need to develop several new skills, besides her natural cooking talent. Sarah wrote down the following missions to get her to her goal:

- Develop skill as blogger
- Become good at photographing food
- Become an accomplished public speaker
- Develop skills in putting together teaching videos
- Develop business and accounting knowledge
- Study at a respected culinary institute

She researched each of these missions and found out what would be required in terms of time and money.

She approached her parents, who were skeptical at first, but after they saw the energy and enthusiasm Sarah had, and after they realized she had done a great deal of quality thinking about the subject, they supported her new direction were happy to work with her on her new educational goals.

As Sarah attended classes, she also created a blog and began developing videos. When she got to the marketing courses she was ready with a number of projects, and developed a cooking course which she sold on the internet, earning her money while she was still going to school. She used the advertising revenue from YouTube™ and the money from her course to pay for some of her education and create more professional products.

Sarah is still in school, completing her business degree, but she has already had many job offers from people that have seen her YouTube™ videos. She has also been contacted by two

> What are the four essential requirements for success?

culinary institutes that have expressed an interest in having her come to their schools. She is currently loving the attention and revising her mission statements.

WHAT IS YOUR VISION?

If you don't already have a vision firmly planted in your mind, take some time now to give it some thought. In this section I will guide you through an exercise to help you explore some possibilities.

In order to simplify and jump start this process, let's divide life into six Vital Realms. You may be able to think of others, or perhaps you don't have a vision in each area. These, like the other examples in this book, are only meant as guides. For each realm, you may eventually develop a clear vision, but for now pick only the ones you care deeply about. You can always come back and add others, or make changes as the situation demands.

The six Vital Realms presented here are:

- Family
- Career
- Financial
- Education
- Spirituality
- Physical Health

Perhaps you already have a vision in mind. You may know that you want to be a good father in a large family, or perhaps you want to be a faithful son and take care of your aging parents. Maybe you want to become a concert pianist or a missionary. Maybe you are a student and just want to get your Bachelor's Degree. If you already have a clear vision in some of these areas, let's start there.

If you don't already have a clear vision, pick one of the Vital Realms, whichever seems most relevant and think about what the greatest achievement you could think of making in that realm.

The Achievement Protocol

HINT: Think about why you purchased this book. You probably already had some vison in mind that you wanted to accomplish.

In the following table, I list a few sample visions for each of the Vital Realms. These are intended to guide you in defining your own, you don't have to select one from this table. Feel free to add another realm if you feel it would be helpful.

On separate Post-It® Notes, write down your chosen realm at the top, then underline it and write your vision below.

> What is the Vital Realm?
>
> What is your vision for this

Visions

Family	Financial	Career	Education	Spirituality	Physical
Be a good parent	Build retirement plan for early retirement	Become an Organic Farmer	Earn MS Degree	Develop Life Long Spiritual Practice	Maintain good lifelong health
Adopt a child	Pay off mortgage	Discover cure for cancer	Become Certified Airplane Mechanic	Understand and embrace lessons of great spiritual leaders	Become Olympic Class Weightlifter
Raise 3 children into happy productive adults	Build Educational Foundation for Scholarships	Become Scuba Instructor	Graduate Cum Laude		Overcome physical limitations
		Become Music Teacher	Learn multiple languages		

Sample of Visions

Vision Summary

The key to achieving a fulfilling life is beginning with a vision that represents the culmination of something that you love, something that you share such an emotional connection with that regardless of setbacks or occasional bumps in the road, you will persevere in an attempt to finally accomplish the vision. A carefully constructed vision will incorporate your core values.

Good visions tend to be broad and sweeping, rather than precise. They describe a final result - the culmination of many separate efforts. They tend not to be constrained by time or by too much precision. At any one time, an individual may have between 1 and 7 visions that they want to seek after over the course of their life. Different visions represent different areas of a person's life. For example, you may have visions relating to physical health, career, education, family, spiritual life, etc. Typically you would want only one vision for any one of these areas.

Remember that as you grow and develop, you may reach a point where you find the original vision has been fulfilled or is no longer relevant. It's ok to change your vision as your life develops or your passion or love becomes clearer to you.

Having a clear vision based on solid core values is essential, but it does not end there. Once you know where you want to go, you need to create a plan that will get you there. In the next section we will discuss how to create the personal missions that will get you to your vision.

The Achievement Protocol

4 MISSIONS

When you discover your mission, you will feel its demand. It will fill you with enthusiasm and a burning desire to get to work on it.

W. Clement Stone

Missions are high-level, strategic efforts consisting of multiple related projects that lead to achieving some part of a vision.

For each Vision you define, you will need to identify a number of missions that will be required to reach that Vision. The exact number is dependent on the vision, but a number between 1 and 8 is typical.

Suppose your vision is to own a small local bakery that supplies bread to local restaurants, your supporting missions might be:

- Obtain necessary business management education or resources
- Obtain necessary baking education
- Develop business plan
- Obtain financial resources for start up
- Obtain building, equipment, and licenses
- Develop customer base

The missions represent the major efforts or programs that are needed for realizing the vision. Each mission must be complete before the vision is realized.

> Can more than one Mission lead to a single Vision?

Each mission will consist of one more projects. The mission completion dates usually occur well into the future because they represent long term efforts that depend on the completion of multiple projects.

When I began studying business in college in the late 1970s, I soon found that I had an affinity for computers that most people did not share. It wasn't long before I realized that one of the key visions in my life was to help people and businesses unleash the power of the technologies that were available to them.

My first mission in attaining that vision was to work for a computer company as a custom programmer for business users. An unexpected opportunity came up before I completed college and in 1978 I began executing that mission. In 1993, after 15 years in the information technology field, I decided it was time to start my own business. I had been developing software applications for small businesses and training users. A couple of years earlier, I had opened a satellite office for a growing computer company, but I was beginning to feel that the company no longer had a vertical path for me to ascend.

I now had a new mission, starting my own business. As I started to seriously consider starting this new business, I reflected on several areas, including:

What scope of services would I offer? I had 15 years of experience in a variety of business environments. I had performed many different services for customers in the past, but now I needed to decide which services I enjoyed doing and what I wanted to offer.

Who would my customers be? Would I target a specific industry or a certain size of business? Would I provide services for home users?

Would I setup an office, or work from my home?

Once I had answers to these and other questions, I defined several new projects which included:
- Develop Business Plan
- Become proficient in new networking technologies
- Become proficient in Windows development tools
- Develop base of satisfied customers
- Create legal business entity

Below is a chart that shows how the missions are connected to the vision and the projects are connected to the mission.

Missions

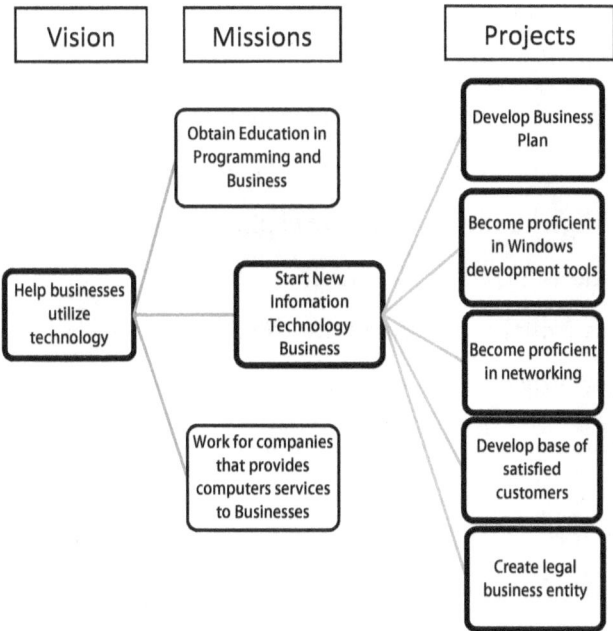

These were among the specific, distinct and focused pillars that were integral to creating a successful business. There were also some administrative pillars, but the above examples are sufficient for this illustration.

Mission Summary

Missions are the key pathways to achieving a vision. They are the first step in bringing your vision down out of the nebulous ether and turning it into concrete reality.

Missions are high-level. They explain what you are going to do to realize your vision, but do not yet have explicit instructions or commitments. These specifics will be addressed in the next section as we consider projects and subprojects.

> Can Missions be changed once started?

5 PROJECTS AND SUBPROJECTS

Even if you are on the right track, you will get run over if you just sit there.

Will Rogers

Projects and subprojects are more specific than missions. To review for a moment, a *mission* is a long-term effort, which when complete directly fulfills a need of a particular *vision*, which is founded on a *core value*. In order to accomplish a *mission*, multiple *projects* will need to be completed, and each of those *projects* may contain *subprojects*. According to the Project Management Institute (2013) a project is defined as an effort having a unique goal and has a specific start and stop date. Missions on the other hand, tend to have a more generalized goal and their completion is often indicated in terms of conditions (such as completion of its projects) or a general timeframe, rather than a particular date. Subprojects are just like projects, with a specific unique goal and a definite start and stop date.

The ultimate goal for a subproject is bring the project to completion. The ultimate goal of the project is to assist in the completion of the mission. And of course ultimate goal of the mission is to help bring about the vision.

Defining Projects

Looking back at the mission I created for my startup Information Technology service business, I identified and initiated several projects to support the mission, including:

- Develop word of mouth marketing from existing customers
- Take classes for various networking products
- Develop relationships with vendors, attend conferences
- Develop relationships with developer organizations
- Create logo and branding materials
- Acquire necessary hardware and software tools
- Establish licensing and accounting relationships

Each of these subprojects directly supports one of the projects as the updated chart on the following page illustrates.

The Achievement Protocol

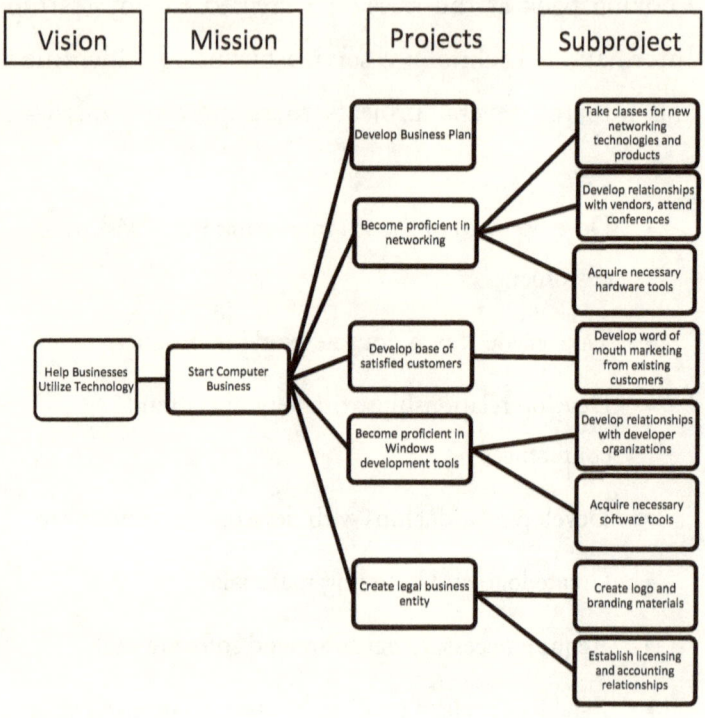

We can see from this chart that all subprojects for a particular project must be complete before that project is complete, all projects must be complete before its respective mission is complete, and when all missions are complete, the vision will be realized.

You will recall that the Project Management Institute (PMI) defines a project as a distinct set of tasks or subprojects with a specific goal, specific start date and specific end date. It is both temporary and unique and is therefore not something routine that is repeated over and over.

Let's take a closer look at just one of the projects identified above, "Become Proficient in Networking". This project is comprised of some subprojects and each of those subprojects will have specific tasks associated with it.

> What is the ultimate aim of a project?

Project: Become Proficient in Networking

Task or Subproject	Start Date	End Date
Learn New Network Technologies	Jan 1, 2014	Mar 15, 2014
Develop Vendor Relationships	Jan 13, 2014	Feb 15, 2014
Purchase Networking Tools	Feb 16, 2014	Mar 15, 2014

These subprojects required multiple tasks in order to complete, and each of the subprojects was partially dependent on the subproject above it. Develop Vendor Relationships first required learning about new network technologies so that some judgments could be made about which vendors were essential.

Itemizing the individual actions steps for subprojects like these is the subject of the next section.

PROJECT SUMMARY

Projects are the most detailed of our planning phases. They can vary greatly in size. A project might be "Take a series of Online Courses on Video Production" which might take 3 weeks to complete. Or a project could be "Earn Adobe Certified Instructor" certification which could take a year depending on the time you have to devote to it.

The scope and timeline of your projects are for you to determine.

6 TASKS

Attempt easy tasks as if they were difficult, and difficult as if they were easy; in the one case that confidence may not fall asleep, in the other that it may not be dismayed.

Baltasar Gracian

As we continue drilling down from the *vision*, which is the broadest and most general expression of our *core values*, on to *missions*, then through *project* and *subprojects*, we ultimately reach *tasks*, which are the most detailed unit of activity. Tasks take us out of the realm of planning where the vision, missions, and projects, live and brings us into the world of action. This is where the rubber meets the road.

Tasks relate directly to both *projects* and *subprojects*. A task is a single item on a to-do list: making a single phone call, writing a single email, taking mail to the post office, making an appointment with an advisor, etc.,.

A project may consist of both tasks and subprojects, which are also comprised of multiple tasks. Tasks have a very short duration, typically between 15 minutes and one day. A task is a direct action that you take. While you can work on multiple projects simultaneously, a task is typically something that occupies 100% of your attention until it is complete.

Throughout the day, we will have many tasks. Some of them will be relevant to projects that we are working on to achieve our vision and some will not. Some tasks will relate directly to a project, some will not.

Not every task that you execute throughout the day will be part of your vision. As you go through the process of living your daily life, it's important to be aware which tasks are integral to building your future and which are not. With this awareness you will be in a better position to prioritize your tasks and ensure that you are spending your time in the most effective way possible in order to create the future of your dreams. You will be able to recognize when your time is being consumed with things that, though they may seem urgent at the moment, actually are not very important in the greater scheme of things.

Even though a task or project is not part of your vision, you can use these same tools to track it so that you can execute more effectively and also be able to review later to see how much of your time is devoted to the pursuit of your vision, and how much is devoted to unrelated work. This information can help you make better decisions about your priorities.

Expanding on our example from the previous section, we will take one of the subprojects from the "Become Proficient in Networking" project and look at the specific tasks in the next section.

EXAMPLES OF TASKS

Let's take look at the subproject called "Develop relationships with vendors…" This required the following tasks in order to complete:

- Apply for Intel Distributorship
- Apply for Tech Data Account
- Apply for CISCO Account
- Setup Microsoft Account
- Create List of potential conferences/training

Each of these tasks is a specific action to be taken and is generally completed in a single sitting. Each is directly aimed at fulfilling the project goal of developing vendor relationships.

> How does a task differ from a project, mission or vision?

Looking at the diagram below, we can see how the individual tasks for "Developing Relationships with Vendors" are related to completed the project of "Becoming Proficient in Networking" which is part of the mission of "Starting a Computer Business", that works toward satisfying the vision of "Helping

Tasks

Businesses Utilize Technology". We can therefore see how the tasks we are performing are linked directly to achieving the ultimate vision.

| Vision | Mission | Proiects | Subprojects | Tasks |

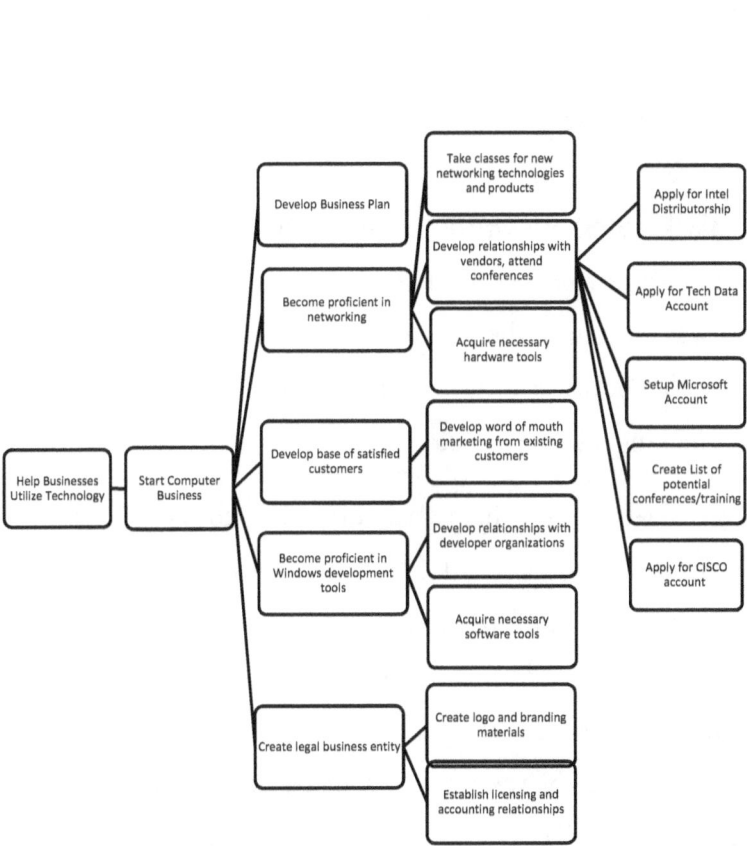

Relationship of tasks to vision

To Do Lists

Perhaps the oldest written form of any management protocol is the "To-Do" list. At first glance, it may be easy to dismiss this tool because of its simplicity, but there can be no doubt of its importance in achievement at all levels and its pervasive use throughout history. One of the earliest written to do lists that I have seen was written about 6,000 years ago. The Hymn to Ninkasi (Black, 1998) was written in ancient Sumerian and listed the specific tasks involved in the process for making beer. It was written in the form of a poem and wasn't terribly concise, however it did list the necessary tasks involved in making a batch of beer.

To-Do lists helps us maintain focus on the immediate tasks at hand. Most of us know how easy it is to get lost in all of the requests or demands on our time. Sometimes the demands are self-imposed, sometimes they are imposed by others, and sometimes they just come up out of the blue as a matter of circumstance. Even with a To-Do list, it can be difficult to stay on track, but it becomes nearly impossible without a list.

With a To-Do list, we can work on each item, one at a time, and check them off as they become complete. If it becomes impossible to complete a task when we intended to, we can transfer it to the front of tomorrow's list.

The actual form of your To-Do list does not need to be fancy. You can use Post-It® Notes, scratch paper, your smart phone or a text editor. It can be as simple as a list of brief descriptions of the task. It doesn't need to be grammatically correct, or comprehensive. This is not a tool for you to communicate with others, rather it is a tool to communicate with yourself. As long as you can understand what it means, that is all that's important.

To-Do List Strategy

When is the best time to create a new To-Do list? The right answer for you will depend on your own style and daily or metabolic rhythm. This should be done, when your head is clear and you are fairly relaxed. Many people find it to be most effective to spend some time at the end of the evening, shortly before going to bed. Take some time to review the status of the tasks accomplished earlier in the day and make the list for the next day, being sure to transfer any unfinished items to the next day's list.

Just before bedtime is a time in the evening when the day's duties are complete and your mind can be cleared for reflection. Taking this time to intentionally reflect on the day you've just completed and the day ahead of you will help you to maintain perspective and will help you see potential problem areas or opportunities and act on them to your advantage.

Standard, simple To-Do lists are great tools, but there is a way to make them even better. Create your list in two columns. In the first column list only those tasks that relate to your specific mission-focused projects. In the second column, list only those tasks that are not directly relevant to a particular mission-focused project. The tasks on the left will lead to the eventual accomplishment of your vision, the tasks on the right,

> Are you in touch with your natural daily rhythms? When are you most productive? Least productive?

although they may be necessary, will not.

During your evening reflection, note where you are spending your time. Ask yourself whether you are moving toward your vision, or away from it.

When you arise in the morning, review your list for the day and get started! As you go through the day, you will come across new tasks. Add them to your task list (preferably at the bottom) or start a new list for tomorrow. The key is to write the task down as soon as you become aware of it. Writing it down will free your mind to focus on the tasks you had committed to for today. If you don't write it down, your mind will continue to nag you about it so you won't forget. Once you've written it down, you can tell the nagging voice to be quiet so you can get some work done.

This point bears repeating, when we are busy and actively engaged in a task, and another task or idea comes along and interrupts us, we need to write down the new task as quickly as possible or we may have difficulty recalling it later. If we tell ourselves we will write it down later, there is a very good chance that we will forget to do so.

If we don't write it down and continue to work through our task, we may experience greater stress in trying not to forget it and in turn will not be able to give proper attention to the task we were initially engaged in.

SARAH'S LIST

The last time we talked about Sarah, she was in college, getting her education, and putting up YouTube™ videos that were getting noticed. She had already received some offers from culinary schools as well as some job offers.

We visit her now and find that she is becoming overwhelmed with all that is happening. Mid-terms are approaching, and one class is a particular concern for her. She has committed to her readers that she would write a new blog entry each week. She also wants to do a more professional looking YouTube™ video on Hollandaise sauce. So far she's just been using the built-in camera on her tablet, but she knows she should put out better work for people to look at. She also wants to finish the latest Suzanne Collins novel before her brother arrives for a visit in two weeks

Instead of going out for drinks on Saturday night, Sarah goes to an all-night diner alone to work on her organization. She starts with the difficult class. She pulls out a sheet of paper and at the top she writes "Biology". She decides that she needs to get an A on the mid-term, so she reviews the syllabus and the subject areas. She decides that she needs to spend two hours a day three times a week doing writing assignments for the class. She also decides she should spend two hours in the library two days a week. She draws a vertical line down the page, about two inches from the left hand margin. At the top of the column, she writes TASKS. She writes two lines below this heading: BIO READ and BIO LIB. She looks at a calendar and next to each line she writes the dates that she is going to assign to each of these tasks. She also records the tasks on her main calendar. Every night she'll look at the task list for the Biology project and make a mark indicating whether she met her commitment or not.

Sarah pulls out a new piece of paper a writes "VIDEO PRODUCTION" at the top. She again draws a vertical line down the left hand side and writes the following tasks in the first column:

- Contact University Catering manager and request possible dates/times to use kitchen
- Contact Jerry and ask if he can video tape and edit the movie
- Gather necessary ingredients, equipment
- Write script for video
- Film video in University Kitchen
- Jerry will edit video
- Meet with Jerry three times during edit process
- Publish final video to YouTube™

Sarah wants to have the video complete in 4 weeks, and Jerry will probably need to have it for up to 10 days so she knows she has to complete her filming in 2 and half weeks. She knows that she'll need about an hour to edit the script. Jerry would like to have two hours in the kitchen to film. She already has most of the ingredients.

Sarah draws another line down the page about an inch to the right of the first line. At the top she labels the column "Duration" and she writes down the time required for Scripting, Filming, and Video Editing.

She draws a third line down the paper and labels the column Start Date.

She knows she needs to contact the Catering Manager and Jerry on Monday, so she writes Monday's date down next to those items. She also makes a notation on her main calendar, where she has already written BIO READ. She puts a small check mark on those items on the task list to remind her that she has put those on the main calendar. Once she makes her calls and gets approval, she can assign dates to the other items.

On another piece of paper, she writes BLOG POST. She reflects on her calendar and other commitments that are not on the calendar and decides that Sunday afternoons are the best time to write. She also knows that she will do some research before writing. She decides that 30 minutes on Wednesday and an hour on Friday should be ample research time.

In the first column labeled TASKS she writes five items

- Conceptualize Topic
- Wednesday Research
- Friday Research
- Write Blog Post
- Publish Blog Post

She makes a column for duration and writes down 30 minutes, 1 hr., and 2 hrs. for Wednesday Research, Friday Research and Write Blog Post, respectively.

She draws another column for Start Date and puts Wednesday's and Friday's dates down. Then she puts Sunday's date down for the Write and Publish tasks. Finally she decides she needs to have her concept no later than Tuesday night so she doesn't stress over it. She writes that date down as well.

She transfers this information to her main calendar, which is starting to look full.

She takes out another piece of paper and writes READING at the top. She looks at the number pages left to read and divides it by the number of days before her brother arrives and concludes that she has to read 30 pages a day to finish it before he arrives.

She writes READ30 in the first column and then writes the date range to the right. Since this is pleasure reading, she doesn't have to be as fastidious in making sure she hits every target date.

Sarah takes a few moments to reflect on whether anything else needs to be considered and decides that she is finished. As she puts everything away, she decides she will write tomorrow's blog on Task Lists and describe her experience this evening...

She puts everything away, and orders a slice of banana cream pie. Knowing that the clutter is on her calendar she can relax and enjoy what's left of the weekend.

Task Summary

The Task is the most detailed level of activity that we have. It represents what we actually DO rather than what we plan. The Vision, Mission, and Projects all represent goals that we want to achieve, but the task is the actual work that gets done to get us there. You can have the most glorious, the most logical, and the most certain, plan ever conceived, but without the active tasks to work steadily toward the goal, the plan will not succeed. This is why the Task is at the bottom level of our pyramid. It forms the foundation, the fundamental unit of achievement, for any level above it.

The follow sections on milestones, roadblocks, reminders, and rewards are all presented to give you the tools you need to make certain that you are successful in your ability to master these tasks which are the *sine qua non* of attaining your vision.

7 MILESTONES

Milestones are markers along the path of a project that help you know that you are making process. They can be setup as frequently as needed in order to keep you motivated. Milestones are intermediate targets to strive for. Having intermediate targets provides us with quicker feedback so we know sooner whether we are on track or not.

Landmark Navigation

When I was in my early teenage years, I joined a Boy Scout troop. We lived in the mountains of Northern Arizona near the Hopi and the Navajo Indian reservations. We were located in the largest Ponderosa Pine forest in the world. My favorite scouting activities included camping, hiking, animal tracking and orienteering, also known as trying not to get lost. One method for staying on track while walking through the forests or deserts was to use landmarks. We would decide what direction we needed to go, then pick three trees or rock formations off in the distance along the line we wanted to travel and walk to it, adding another landmark as we reached each one, so we always had a trail of three visible landmarks to follow.

This kept us moving on the right path and assured that as long as we were reaching the landmarks we were aiming for, we would eventually find our ultimate target.

Milestones work just that way for our projects. As long as we are getting to the milestones were aiming for, at the time that we're aiming for, we know we're on track. If we reach the milestone, but we're later than we expected, we know that we either need to pick up speed or adjust our deadline.

MILESTONE SPACING

The exact spacing or pacing of your milestones is a matter of personal choice and depends on the nature and length of the project. As you start this process, you might want to keep your milestones fairly close together, then as you become more comfortable with your pacing, adjust them leaving more space between them.

> What Milestones have you been using in your life?

Ideally, your milestones will be spaced such that reaching each one will be challenging, but attainable with some effort.

MILESTONE SUMMARY

Milestones exist to keep you on track and keep you focused on reaching your goal, whether your goal is the completion of a project, mission or attainment of a vision.

By setting milestones, we reduce the tendency to wander off in the wrong the direction. Milestones help to provide us with positive feedback, assuring us that we are still on the road that we know will lead to our goal.

So what happens when you reach the milestone? You get a reward, of course! And that is the subject of our next topic.

8 REWARDS

An important concept in motivational psychology is incentivizing desired outcomes, where a desired result is rewarded in order to encourage task completion. In *Goal Setting and Task Management* (1990), Locke and Latham show that rewards (both intrinsic and external) are an integral part of the High Performance Cycle, enhancing satisfactions and impelling one on to setting additional goals.

If you are having trouble reaching your milestones or completing your projects, institute a reward system. What sort of reward? How about, when you reach that next milestone, you'll have a cup of tea and read for 15 minutes. Or call up a friend and take them out to a spontaneous lunch, or buy a new lure for your fishing rod. Or you can take your wife out to a special dinner.

It doesn't have to be a big, expensive, or complicated reward. It can be very simple, as long as it is something that you like and something that you will look forward to.

Now this may sound like a bribe, but that is only because it *is* a bribe. It just adds a little bit of fun motivation to keep you focused on reaching that next point.

As I write the book that you are now reading, I have set for myself certain milestones concerning number of words written, completing certain sections, etc. Some of the rewards I've chosen are: taking time out for a long walk, going to Starbucks for a special drink, watching a movie that I've been wanting to see.

> Can Missions be changed once started?

Delayed Gratification

The real magic in setting intermediate rewards like this is not that you accomplish a particular task, but what you achieve by practicing intentional delayed gratification.

The ability to delay gratification, to wait to receive your reward, has been shown to have a high correlation with success. Walter Mischel, a professor at Stanford University, performed what came to be known as *marshmallow experiments* in the late '60's and early '70's.

He tested children and allowed them to choose a treat, either a marshmallow, a cookie, or a pretzel. They were told that they could eat their treat now, but if they waited for 15 minutes or so they could have two treats instead of one. Most of the children struggled with the challenge, battling temptation and sometimes going through agonizing physical movements to keep from eating the treat that was sitting in front of them. Some just gave in and ate the treat immediately, some managed to the end without eating it, and some gave in to temptation after struggling for a while (Mischel 1972).

18 years later they looked at the same children and found there was a strong correlation between those that were able to wait for their treat, and their later success in school and in general competence (Shoda 1990).

Similar studies have been done that show the same correlation. Self-control and self-discipline, as demonstrated by the ability to delay gratification is an important component in any endeavor and a good predictor of success. By setting milestones and placing rewards that encourage us to persevere until that milestone is reached, we can exercise our self-control and develop a quality that will ultimately lead to greater success in the pursuit of our vision.

Reward Summary

Rewarding yourself for staying on track and making regular progress is a fun way to accomplish what you are working on now, and also to build the qualities that will help in the future. As you become good at hitting your milestones and earning your rewards, extend them so that you have to push yourself even harder for a longer amount of time before you get rewards.

Be persistent in the way you go about accomplishing the things on your task list and you see the benefits very quickly as you begin to accomplish more in a few hours than you previously accomplished in days.

You may now be wondering, with all of the things you now have to think about, projects, tasks, milestones, rewards, etc., how are you going to stay on top of them? That is the subject of our next topic, Reminders.

The Achievement Protocol

9 REMINDERS

By now you have probably realized 2 things about the system that is presented in this book:

- This system is logical and powerful
- You may need some help keeping up with all of the tracking requirements

Enter the Reminder system.

In order to make sure that this system doesn't get lost in the shuffle after the third or fourth day, we will create some reminders to keep us from getting behind.

In the appendix I will have some forms for you to use and a manual method for Reminders, but if you have a smartphone, tablet computer, laptop or desktop computer, it would be much better to setup reminders within one of your applications so that it will automatically pop up at the appointed time.

Choose a method or technology that works for you. What is important is not whether it's a smartphone, a smartwatch, a kitchen timer or a notepad. Find a method or technology that will work reliably for you.

Productivity Reminders

Productivity Reminders let you know of upcoming deadlines. They are normally associated with tasks, subprojects and projects.

When you choose a deadline for any of these entities, you also set one or more reminders to rattle your cage, so to speak, as the deadline approaches so you can make sure you're on track.

If you have these setup on an electronic device, you'll see an alert or hear an alarm. If you have this reminder in a manual paper tracking system, then you will need to review your reminders on a regular basis.

In either case, once you've been reminded of the upcoming deadline, take a moment to take stock of your progress and decide whether you're going to meet the deadline. If it looks like you're getting behind, you have two options. If you are able, put some extra effort into it to meet the deadline. If there's no way to meet it, change the deadline and setup new reminders. It's a good idea to keep a note of the original deadline so that you can look back over the project and see what deadlines had to be extended and why.

ROUTINE REMINDERS

Routine reminders are not related to a specific project or task. Instead they are tied to a time of day, day of week, day of month, etc. They remind us to do things that we need to do regularly, regardless of what projects or tasks we are currently working on.

For example, when we are getting started with this process, we may need reminders in the evening to attend to our To-Do lists and prepare for tomorrow's activity. If you're like me and have a difficult time getting your brain in gear in the morning, you might want to set a timer to remind you to check your To-Do list in the morning.

On a regular basis, let's say once or twice a month, you should take a high level look at your projects and estimate the percentage of completion, then do the same with your missions. In the appendix I've included a link to a spreadsheet file that you can use that will help you log this

> What is the difference between a Productivity Reminder and a Routine Reminder?

information over time so that you can graphically see your progress.

The frequency you use for setting up the Routine Reminders is up to you and needs to be consistent with your projects and missions.

TICKLER FILE

The Tickler File is an old-school reminder system for those who prefer a pencil and paper based solution. It consists of a file – usually an index card file, with 43 dividers, 31 for the days of the month, and 12 for the months of the year.

If you want to remind yourself about something that is coming up later in the current month, you write a note and file it at the appropriate date. Each morning you go to the current date, and look at everything in your tickler file. If you want to keep a reminder for something that is occurring after the current month, you file it in the relevant month. When the current month is over, you go through the items in next month's folder and distribute to their appropriate days.

The Tickler File system can be a very powerful to method to relieve the stress of having to keep so many things in mind and allow you to focus on the present moment rather than expending your energy being concerned about future commitments.

REMINDER SUMMARY

When there are a lot of demands made on our time, when we feel like we are being pulled in many directions, it can be difficult to keep track of everything that needs to be done. If we lose focus on working toward what we really want, we will not have more time. Instead all of our time and energy will be spent doing things that will not lead to our ultimate vision. We need to learn to guard our time jealously and realize that we have the right and the duty to say, "Sorry, I don't have time to do that for you today, but if you still need my help next week, I'm free for a couple of hours then." Ultimately by focusing on attaining our vision we are going to be providing more value to others, than if we squander our time taking care of every urgent demand that arises.

The Achievement Protocol

10 ROADBLOCKS

On the path to success, there is one thing that you can count on encountering: Roadblocks. We are certain to be challenged at various points along the way. Generally, these roadblocks can be viewed as learning experiences for us. Though they may be painful and inconvenient we need to anticipate them so that when we do encounter them, we are able to deal with them thoughtfully and not allow them to prevent us from achieving our goals.

In this section, we'll take a look at some of the roadblocks that you are likely to run into and ways of dealing with them in a productive fashion.

CHOOSING THE WRONG VISION

One of the main purposes of this book is to show you how you can achieve a fulfilling and satisfying life by systematically doing the things that will assist you in realizing your vision. To realize self-actualization.

If the vision you set out to achieve is not authentically yours, then you will not be fulfilled or satisfied, even if you achieve it. Make sure the vision that you have as your target, is your own. That it comes from your heart, not from well-meaning friends or family, not from society, but from the core of your own being.

In a personal discussion with Dr. Locke, he shared with me some unpublished excerpts of an upcoming work on the subject of burnout in which he states that having the wrong goal (or vision) can not only be frustrating and unfulfilling, but can have a variety of detrimental effects on our mental, emotional, physical and psychological states. He further suggests that your vision meet four criteria. Your vision should reflect: a) what you truly enjoy, b) your true passions, c) what you want for yourself, and d) the type of person you want to be.

Early on in this book, I encouraged you to take your time and come up with good core values that represent what is truly important to you. If you shortcut this process and use someone else's core values, or pick core values that you think you 'should' have, you will be doing yourself a great disservice.

Take your time defining your core values and your visions. You have the rest of your life to work on them and the time you spend in making sure they truly represent your heart's desire, the happier you will be in their pursuit.

LIFE IS ORGANIC

As important as it is to find your authentic vision and core values, it is also important to recognize that life is organic. Regardless of how well we plan, life grows in sometimes unexpected ways. It rarely proceeds in a straight line with no diversions.

The 18th century Scottish poet Robert Burns wrote a poem that included a line that is usually translated,

The best laid plans of mice and men often go awry.

Robert Burns

In the poem, "To a Mouse", Burns (1787) was apologizing to a mouse whose nest he had just run over with his plow. In his apology he reflected on the fact that it is as true with mice as it is with men, that we can create meticulous plans for our lives, only to have them overturned in a moment due to circumstances beyond our control and foresight.

It is certainly not unusual for changing conditions to render a specific plan irrelevant. This happens most often with plans that are not linked to a specific vision, however even our vision can ultimately change. Understanding our contribution to the world, our destiny, our unique vision is something that can take years of false starts and half steps before we truly understand ourselves well enough to know what we must do.

A 19th century German Field Marshall said,

No plan survives contact with the enemy.

Moltke the Elder

While life is certainly not our enemy, this saying is true for life as well. Perhaps for our purpose here, we should change the object "enemy" to "reality". We can plan every moment for the next twenty years in great detail, but something can come along in a heartbeat that will change our course forever. A chance encounter with someone that inspires us to go into a better direction, a sudden and unexpected illness, or loss of a loved one, new opportunities that you were never aware of, a realization that assumptions you had previously made are false, etc. There are many things that can happen that will alter our core values, which in turn will change the relevance of certain visions.

Once we set a vision and begin working toward it, we need to recognize that there may come a point as we grow and as the world around us changes, when we need to adjust our vision or choose a different vision in order to attain the fulfillment and satisfaction that we seek.

Stress

> *It's not the load that breaks you down, it's the way you carry it.*
>
> Lou Holtz

When we discuss stress as a problem or roadblock, it's helpful for us to first understand stress at a very fundamental level. We will see that stress is not always bad, in fact in can be beneficial and even indispensable to growth. Understanding stress will help us to manage it effectively.

Stress occurs when opposing forces are applied to something. These opposing forces are often external, but they can be internal as well. Stress generally results in some change occurring.

Stress is something that we all have been subjected to since the very moment of our conception. Immediately cells in the previously unfertilized and dormant egg began dividing. This cellular division, known as *mitosis*, is the result of processes that cause internal stress within the cell, forcing it to split into two. Without the process of mitosis causing this internal stress within each cell, a process which occurs trillions of times every day in our bodies, there would be no growth and we could not exist.

Our muscles also benefit from stress, which is why we exercise. By stressing our muscles, we know that they breakdown, then rebuild and become stronger. The rebuilding process involves using proteins to recreate and rebuild the muscle. Micah Drummond found that by ingesting certain amino acids, we make it easier for our muscles to use the protein and supercharge the rebuilding process. (Drummond, 2009)

In 2013, Jane Brody published an article in the New York Times discussing the effects that stressing our bones has on our skeletal structure. She reported that activities like swimming or cycling, which do not produce stress on the skeleton do not have the same bone strengthening effect as walking or running. (Brody 2013)

We see, then, that stress can be useful and vital in many ways. This is true in our lives as well as our physiology. When we are stressed by something, there are forces that are acting upon us. If we seek to understand what it is about the situation or about us that is causing us to be stressed, we can often find an answer that will leave us stronger.

I once worked with a person that caused me an unusual amount of stress. It seemed that there was constant, unhealthy tension between us, despite my best efforts to work productively with her. After allowing the stress to bother me for too long, I decided to try to understand it. I reflected on my world view, and then thought about her world view, I began to see how certain things that I did were unwitting triggers for her and I was unintentionally putting her in a defensive position. And of course she was reacting defensively. I changed my approach to my interactions with her, and started anticipating ways that she might misunderstand me. I soon began to have a more productive relationship with her. I also learned about some of my own potential blind spots and now have a way to avoid inadvertently causing myself more stress in certain areas.

What most successful people learn is that stress is a sign that there is an energetic force at work. We can choose to submit to the force and crumble beneath it, or we can harness it and channel it into a productive direction.

I originally learned that lesson when I 10 years old. I studied Judo for a couple of years and one of the key principles of that martial art is based on the knowledge that your opponent will bring a lot of energy and momentum to try to defeat you. By simply redirecting the energy and momentum that they are bringing to you, you can defeat the opponent, even one that is much larger and much stronger than you.

It would be several years before I understood that the same principle can be applied in many areas of life.

Norman Vincent Peale, author of the excellent book *Power of Positive Thinking*, said it this way:

> *Every problem contains the seeds of its own solution. If you don't have any problems, you don't get any seeds.*
>
> *Norman Vincent Peale*

Sometimes the cause of the stress that we experience is not an external force. Sometimes stress is caused internally. In 1927, researching psychologists identified a particular type of stress that came to be known as the Zeigarnik Effect. Bluma Zeigarnik and a team of Russian psychologists were studying how memory was affected by a busy mind and by multiple interruptions that caused some tasks to be left undone so that other tasks could be pursued (Zeigarnik 1927).

The Zeigarnik Effect describes the fact that when we are forced to move away from tasks without completing them, there is a natural mechanism in the mind to remind us of those unfinished tasks. Unfortunately, this natural reminder is not very effective because it usually occurs when we are busy with something else, disrupting our current work and causing us to worry for a moment about the unfinished tasks. Then we struggle trying to get back up to speed on the task at hand. All of which produces – you guessed it – stress!

This is why it is so important to write down and reschedule your unfinished tasks as quickly as possible. Your mind will accept that you are doing something about it and stop reminding you at inconvenient times.

The next time you feel stressed, ask yourself whether there is a better way to carry your load, or whether the cause of the stress can be redirected in a positive way.

The organizational tools in this book, particularly the To-Do list, will help alleviate some of the internal stress from your life.

FEAR OF FAILURE

It is impossible to live without failing at something, unless you live so cautiously that you might as well not have lived at all, in which case you have failed by default.

J. K. Rowling

One of the most basic fears that can create obstacles to our success is the Fear of Failure. This fear petrifies many people and causes them to stop, or never start, attempting to achieve their hearts desire. In truth, failure is something to be embraced. Failure can teach us many lessons. Lessons about ourselves, our methods, our endeavors. Success almost always comes after failure. Not after every failure, mind you, but after we have failed enough times, learned from our mistakes, regrouped and made necessary adjustments, then proceeded again.

Failure by its nature is an event, but many people think of it as a permanent state of being. Failure is something that happens. It is not a state of being until we decide to allow it to be. All successful people have failed, and many successful people will fail again. The difference between someone that we consider successful and someone we consider a failure, is that the successful person picked herself up, dusted herself off, then went back to trying to succeed. The person that appears to be a failure, chose not to continue trying.

FEAR OF SUCCESS

> *We fear our highest possibilities (as well as our lowest ones). We are generally afraid to become that which we can glimpse in our most perfect moments, under the most perfect conditions, under conditions of great courage. We enjoy and even thrill to the godlike possibilities we see in ourselves in such peak moments. And yet we simultaneously shiver with weakness, awe, and fear before these very same possibilities.*
>
> *Dr. Abraham Maslow*

Fear of Success is a close second to Fear of Failure. It is just as detrimental to our progress. Fear of success comes from an uncertainty in our ability to live up to future expectations.

We may fear that by achieving our goal, we will be held to an even higher standard that we may not be equal to. We may fear that once we achieve our goal, we will lose friends or things that are comfortable for us right now.

This fear is not entirely unfounded. It is common for someone on an intentional path of achieving success through personal development to find that their friends are not as supportive as they ought to be. Rather than wanting you to be successful, they may do things to discourage you. This behavior usually stems from a fear that they have. If you demonstrate to your peers that you can achieve at will, they will not have any excuse not to do the same. Sadly, many people in our culture are comfortable labelling themselves as victims. They have difficulty abandoning the comfortable thought that some condition, person or group is keeping them from being successful. They are unwilling to do the hard work necessary, but rather than admit to that, they make someone else responsible for their unremarkable, unfulfilled life.

It may be difficult, but it is imperative that we overcome this fear and accept that becoming more than we currently are will mean making changes that will include breaking away from those people, circumstances or beliefs that hold us back and prevent us from living a fulfilled life. This means that we will necessarily need to move outside our comfort zone and boldly face new challenges and new experiences.

Fear of Criticism

Similar to the Fear of Failure, the Fear of Criticism stops us from doing anything different that might stand out simply because someone might tell us they don't like it or don't like something about it. This is a very difficult fear to overcome.

No matter what it is that we do, there will be some that approve, and others that do not. If you have self-doubt, you will listen only to those that do not approve, and you will dismiss the opinions of those that do approve as being biased or insincere.

If you are self-confident, on the other hand, the opposite will be true: you will listen most to those that approve, and rather than be hurt by those that criticize you, you will examine the criticism to see if any of it is useful, then dismiss the rest.

The Achievement Protocol

Time Flies

Tempus Fugit is a phrase found on the face of many clocks and is usually translated as "Time Flies". This seems to imply that Time goes by quickly.

But *fugit* is Latin and actually means to flee or escape. It is the root for the word *fugitive*, so the phrase actually means Time Escapes.

Escapes from what? It escapes from whoever has it, of course. It escapes from me, it escapes from you. In other words whatever time we have is making a break for it, it is fleeing from us.

But what is the time that you or I have? Can you truthfully say you have the future? Isn't it really true that the future is something that we only hope will come to us?

Do you really have time that is past? Or do you only have memories of things that were once present? As quickly as the future becomes the present, the present becomes the past.

The only time that any of us actually have, that we can do anything with; the only time that we can use to accomplish any task or work toward the achievement of any vision; the only time that can escape us, is the present moment.

One of the simplest and most powerful tips I learned in my journey was to develop the habit of asking one question throughout the day. Whether I'm busy or relaxing, whether I'm driving or dozing, this one question will waft through my thoughts: Am I making the most productive use of my time right now?

I don't want you to misunderstand, sometimes relaxing and dozing are indeed the most productive use of your time. Sometimes we need to take a break and recharge. Or just take some time out and be spontaneous. We need to do this not only for ourselves, but also for others as well. The key is to be cognizant of whether your current activities are likely to bring you closer to your goal or farther away.

As you go through your day, bear in mind that the only moment you have is the present one. What will you do with that moment before it escapes?

ROADBLOCK SUMMARY

There will be external obstacles that we face as we go through this process. Some will be surmountable. Some may force us to redirect. But the biggest obstacles that people face are not external.

If we are not sufficiently clear about our vision, its achievement is not likely to be fulfilling to us.

Failure is natural. It is simply an event that occurs. If we persist even after failure and seek to learn its lessons, then we will eventually succeed.

We need to be aware of the potential fears that we that could halt our progress. We don't have to let them stop us. The courageous that forge ahead in the face of danger, do so in spite of the fear they may experience. They know that the ultimate goal is too important to allow something like fear stop them from achieving it.

> Is Failure a choice that people make? Why would anyone choose to fail?

The Chinese *Book of Changes*, the I Ching, tells us that righteous pursuit brings reward. Ensure that your missions and visions are good for others as well as yourself and your courageous persistence will be rewarded.

Ask yourself from time to time whether the activity that you are engaged in is moving you closer to, or farther from your goal. The only moment you have, at any given time is the present one. Use it thoughtfully and intentionally.

There will be times on your journey down this *Road Less Traveled*, that the path ahead of you seems impossible. The challenges, as difficult as they seem, are not insurmountable. We discuss *Desperation and Inspiration* in the next chapter.

11 DESPERATION & INSPIRATION

DESPERATION

Up to this point we have looked at the specific methodology that you can use to attain your vision. If you consistently follow this methodology, you will reach your goal. But life can be tricky.

Henry David Thoreau once wrote that "The mass of men are leading lives of quiet desperation." In other words, we look around us and we see other people that appear to be content. But if we were to be able to know their hearts, we would be able to see that what seems like contentment is often just settling for less than they are capable of. And even though they don't mention having dreams or ambitions that are far away from where they are currently heading, they have them still and in the quiet moments of the night, they think about them and wish they had made other choices in life.

Since we don't know what they are actually thinking, it's natural to look upon others and think, "If only I had a life like they have, I could be as happy as they are."

I'm reminded of a beautiful poem by Max Ehrmann (1927). A framed copy of this poem hangs by my front door and I see it each time I come home and each time I leave the house. It is a scant 312 words that is packed with the most sublime wisdom. One of the lines in the poem is:

> *If you compare yourself with others, you may*
> *become vain and bitter;*
> *For always there will be greater or lesser*
> *persons than yourself.*
>
> *Max Ehrmann*

It is better to recognize that other people have their paths, just as you have your own. And when we compare ourselves with someone else, we may actually be looking only at what they want us to see. So avoid this particular trap and do not allow someone else's circumstances, real or perceived, to affect the way you feel about your progress.

And speaking of progress. While we would all like to think that the *Road Less Traveled*, the one that we are on, is smooth and straight and level, the fact is that, even though it can be all of those things sometimes, it can't be all of those things all of the time. There will be struggles and uphill battles that need to be fought and won.

As you make progress toward your goal, you may experience what mystics have referred to as the "Dark Night of the Soul". This is a period that tests us and can be quite difficult. During this period, it can be easy to lose faith and want to give up. Nothing seems to be going in your favor. You begin to question whether you ever should have chosen this path.

Be patient. You have the strength to persevere and see it through, even though it may not always feel that way.

The Achievement Protocol

INSPIRATION

One of the techniques that you can use to gird yourself against the negative effects of the "Dark Night" or those times when you seem to be hitting a series of rough spots in the road, is to prepare yourself with inspirational thoughts that you can recall, like candles to light your path and keep you from getting lost.

There are many inspirational quote of the day sites or apps that you can sign up for and have daily quotes emailed to you or sent to your mobile device. I suggest creating a file for the quotes that particularly speak to you. Then when you feel you may be slipping into that quite desperation, you can look through your file and be reminded of the many lights that burn so brightly in the world.

There are books, scriptures, or devotionals that you can keep close at hand for boosts of inspiration. Many people find that a morning reading of such a book can set the stage for a positive day. Combined with a meditation or prayer period, such a routine can have lasting positive benefits.

DESPERATION AND INSPIRATION SUMMARY

One reason that we feel desperate when we are in times of turmoil is that we feel alone, as though we are the only ones that are suffering through these travails. It is helpful, and truthful, to recognize that we are not alone. We are neither the only ones suffering, nor are we the only ones that can help carry our burden. Look to other sources of inspiration, whether they are friends, relatives, or people that lived thousands of years before you. Remember that the struggles you are having are not as unique as they may seem, and comfort is not as far away as you may suppose.

Use inspiration, first as a shield, then as a weapon, against desperation. Though our path be dark, there may yet be lights just above the horizon to guide us. Lift up your eyes and your heart and find them.

CONCLUSION

A cursory review of existing popular literature on goal setting and achievement might lead one to conclude that this is largely a metaphysical art. There are many good books that will instruct you on how to use meditation and creative visualization to bring about changes in your reality, to attain your ultimate vision.

While I acknowledge the value that much of that advice has, many of these books fall short in presenting a practical tactical plan for achievement. I am convinced that a good plan, well executed, will help your realize your vision most efficiently. Meditation and visualization may also have an important role in your life. Internal tools such as these can help overcome fears, break bad habits, develop good habits, and keep you spiritually and emotionally centered. They can assist you in finding the right vision or mission to seek after or help provide the answer to particular problems you might encounter. They can provide insights of incalculable value to aid you in achieving your vision. The strategy and tools outlined in this book augment those metaphysical efforts and transfer the responsibility for action out of the mystical realm and into the hands of the reader.

In formal Project Management, there are many planning, tracking, and communication tools that are not discussed in this book. Most of the omissions are due to the fact that the strategy presented here is an intimately personal strategy, while many of the components of formal Project Management are tools that are primarily designed to communicate aspects of the project status with other people. Since the reader is the only stakeholder and likewise the only human resource, only those aspects that are essential for accomplishment have been included.

If you apply the Achievement Protocol laid out in the forgoing pages of this book you will find that you are able to accomplish more, with less stress and less frustration. You will enjoy all of the benefits of knowing that you are able to spend your time being true to your highest nature without having to compromise between having a job that pays the bills and following your passion.

This knowledge will ultimately free you to become the complete person that you are meant to be, to not only reach a fulfilled life, but to live a life fulfilled.

The Achievement Protocol

AFTERWORD
BY WAYNE HOUCHIN

A few years ago I was in London filming a TV series about magic and science. The flat I was staying in was a charming one-bedroom on a quiet street just outside the city. There was a café and a used bookshop next door and the train station was a short walk around the corner. It was lovely.

The show I was working on was a science show cleverly disguised to look like a magic show. We created and performed incredible magic effects all over the world that were entirely made possible by science. In one episode we used light and sound to create the illusion that water was levitating upwards. In another we used a sound-frequency only heard by children to create the illusion of super-human memory. Each episode allowed us to talk about and explore incredible scientific principles, some of which turned out to be quite dangerous.

One night I was startled awake by a phone call from one of my producers. They had been filming a large stunt with one of the other performers and something had gone wrong. James had been injured during the stunt and was being taken to the hospital. I forget the exact words, but the next part of our conversation went something like:

Producer: James is fine, but his arm is a bit hurt. He's supposed to film another stunt soon, but because he's injured he won't be able to do it. Will you do it in his place?

Me: What's the stunt?

Producer: A bungee jump.

Me: I've never done that before. What's the angle?

Producer: We're going to cut the bungee cord in half.

Me: And then?

Producer: You jump.

Me: With the cord cut in half?

Producer: Yes.

Me: How do I not also end up in the hospital?

Producer: A phonebook.

Me: ...

My producer explained things, I thought about it and said yes. I got up, made coffee, and began to study the science. I didn't sleep.

Less than 48 hours later, I was standing on a small platform 165 feet above pavement, a live audience gazing up at me from below. Almost a dozen high-definition cameras were pointed at me including one mounted on a remote controlled drone hovering in the distance. In the window of a high-rise next to the crane that was holding our platform stood a naked man sipping a cup of tea. Watching.

Attached to my ankles was a bungee cord that had been cut in half. A phonebook was then attached to each half, the pages of each book were then interwoven: a page from one book, then a page from the other. The science says that the friction of the pages touching each other should be enough to prevent them from separating. So, the books *should* stick to each other and prevent me from falling to my death.

Theoretically.

The crowd down below began to shout, "10, 9, 8, 7..."
As they counted down, I couldn't help but wonder, "How the hell did I end up here?"

...

I've been interested in magic since I was a kid. My Dad showed me my first magic trick and I was hooked. When I was 16, I booked myself into a small theater and my Dad helped me organize a large publicity stunt to promote it. I made the front page of the newspaper, sold out the theater, and learned that I could have big dreams and big ambitions. My parents taught me to *play*, then taught me to *play* with purpose. As my Dad developed the tools and systems now in this book, he shared them with me. I was lucky.

Throughout my career, I've used various parts of his system to organize my *play* in order to accomplish things I dreamed of as a kid and ultimately, that's how I ended up hosting a TV show doing insanely dangerous things.

...

The naked man in the window was still watching and I was shaking. The audience below was shouting, "6, 5, 4, 3..."

Loudspeakers amplified their shouts and my heart skipped a beat. I looked out across London, the view was stunning, and fell forward.

Gravity pulled me down and I lost my breath. But then, I felt a gentle tug on my feet and a gradual slow in my fall and I bounced upwards! The books held, the science worked, and the bungee jump was a success. Truly one of the most thrilling moments of my life.

Hindsight being 20/20, it's obvious that the values, ideas, and philosophy my Dad instilled in me are directly responsible for the adventures I've found myself on, and he's shared much of that wisdom in this book. Use these techniques to organize your *play*. *Play* with purpose and vision and live your dream.

Wayne Houchin

INDEX

A

artificial limitation	8

B

Baltasar Gracian	49
Bandura, Albert	9
beer	20, 54
budget	23, 26

C

chocolate	20
comfort zone	8
confirmation-bias	10
Core values	5

D

DEFINITIONS	xxxvii
Delayed Gratification	71

E

Envelope System	24

F

fleas	8
Ford, Henry	9

G

Gandhi, Mahatma	5

J

jar of fleas	8

L

Landmark Navigation	65
limitations	8
Locke, Edwin	xix, 69, 84, 128

M

Manage Earnings	23
marshmallow experiments	
self-control	71
Milestone Spacing	67
Milestones	65
Mischel	71
mission	37

O

orienteering	66

P

Passion	16, 19
projects	43

R

Relationship of tasks to vision	53
Reward	73
rhythm	55

S

Sarah	58
Self-control	72
self-efficacy	9
Shoda	72

T

Tasks	49
Tasks Examples	52
temptation	71
TIPS FOR SUCCESS	xxxi

V

video games	20
Vital Realms	31

APPENDIX

The forms in this section will help you become organized in the way that you execute and document your tasks. I recommend that you begin by using them as described for at least a month.

After using these forms for a while, you may find that your effectiveness can be increased by making subtle changes to the ways that the forms are used. The goal is to make you most effective.

Use the following forms as long as they can help you:

- Vision Worksheet
- Mission Worksheet
- Project Task List
- Evening Review
- Daily To-Do List
- Tracking Spreadsheet

VISION WORKSHEET

Vision Worksheet
DATE STARTED
REALM
Core Values: (List them in this box)
Vision: (Describe the Vision in this box)

The Achievement Protocol

MISSION WORKSHEET

Mission Worksheet
DATE STARTED
Mission: (Describe the Mission in this box)
Notes

PROJECT TASK LIST

Project Name	
Deadline	
Mission Name	
Vision	

Task Name	Duration	Start Date	Stop Date	Status

For each project, whether it is related to a vital mission or not, complete this form and list all the tasks or subprojects that will be required to complete it.

Evening Review

At the end of the day, list the tasks that you have completed and note the time spent on each task. You may choose to use your To-Do List and place a check mark and the time spent directly on it.

At the same time, make a notation on your Project Task list, noting the time spent and whether or not it is complete.

As you complete a project, make a note on the related Mission Worksheet that the project is complete and note the total time spent on the project.

DAILY TO-DO LIST

At the end of the day, create your To-Do list for the next day. Transfer the items you were unable to complete today over to tomorrow's To-Do list or assign them a different date and put them into a tickler system.

Use the form on the following page or create your own. Whatever form or format you choose, the key is to use it consistently.

The Achievement Protocol

Daily To-Do List

Date		
Project Name	Task Name	Status
ANTICIPATIONS	(Things I'm waiting on)	
Person	Task	Status

Progress Tracking

Please visit the following link for resources that will help you keep track of your progress.

http://AchievementProtocol.AdHocPress.com/Tracking

Sign up at: http://**bonus**.adhocpress.com/sign-up for exclusive offers, opportunities, and resources for creating a better life.

REFERENCES

Bandura, A. (2013). The role of self-efficacy in goal-based motivation. In E.A. Locke & G.P Latham (Ed.). Development in goal setting and task performance. (pp. 147-157) New York: Taylor & Francis.

Black, J.A., Cunningham, G., Ebeling, J., Flückiger-Hawker, E., Robson, E., Taylor, J., and Zólyomi, G., The Electronic Text Corpus of Sumerian Literature (http://etcsl.orinst.ox.ac.uk/), Oxford 1998–2006. Hymn to Ninkasi Retrieved from http://etcsl.orinst.ox.ac.uk/cgi-bin/etcsl.cgi?text=t.4.23.1&display=Crit&charenc=gcirc&lineid=t4231.p1#t4231.p1 December 20, 2014

Brody, J. (2013) Building up bones with a little bashing. Retrieved from http://well.blogs.nytimes.com/2013/08/12/building-up-bones-with-a-little-bashing/?_r=0 December 20, 2014

Burns, R. (1787). Poems, chiefly in the Scottish dialect By Robert Burns. Dublin: Printed for William Gilbert.

Drummond, M.J., et al. (2009)/ Journal of Applied Physiology Vol. 106 no. 4, 1374-1384 DOI: 10.1152/japplphysiol.91397.2008

Ehrmann, M. (1927). Desiderata. Retrieved from http://www.sfheart.com/desiderata.html, December 30, 2014

Locke, E., & Latham, G. (1990). A theory of goal setting & task performance. Englewood Cliffs, N.J.: Prentice Hall.

Mischel, Walter; Ebbesen, Ebbe B.; Raskoff Zeiss, Antonette (1972). "Cognitive and attentional mechanisms in delay of gratification.". Journal of Personality and Social Psychology 21 (2): 204–218. doi:10.1037/h0032198

Maslow, A.H. Synanon & eupsychia Journal of Humanistic Psychology, 1967, 1, 28-35

Maslow, A. H. Theory of metamotivation: The biological rooting of the value-life. Journal of Humanistic Psychology October 1967 vol. 7 no. 2 93-127

Shoda, Yuichi; Mischel, Walter; Peake, Philip K. (1990). "Predicting Adolescent Cognitive and Self-Regulatory Competencies from Preschool Delay of Gratification: Identifying Diagnostic Conditions". Developmental Psychology 26 (6): 978–986. doi:10.1037/0012-1649.26.6.978

Moltke, Helmuth, Graf von, Militarische Werke. vol. 2, part 2., pp. 33-40. Found in Hughes, Daniel J. (ed.) Moltke on the Art of War: selected writings. (1993). Presidio Press: New York, New York. ISBN 0-89141-575-0. p. 45-47

PMI 2013. Project management body of knowledge. Newtown, Pennsylvania: Project Management Institute

Zeigarnik, B. (1927): Das Behalten erledigter und unerledigter Handlungen. Psychologische Forschung 9, 1-85.

Ziglar, Z. (1974). Biscuits, fleas, and pump handles. Gretna: Pelican Pub. Co..

www.ingramcontent.com/pod-product-compliance
Lightning Source LLC
Chambersburg PA
CBHW030443300426
44112CB00009B/1141